JOHN LOCKE
(1632—1704)

C000265187

THE ADAMSON LECTURE
for 1932

by

NORMAN KEMP SMITH, D.Litt., LL.D., F.B.A.
Professor of Logic and Metaphysics in the University of Edinburgh

MANCHESTER UNIVERSITY PRESS
1933

JOHN LOCKE

(1632–1704)

PLATO has suggested that action is so much more natural to us than contemplation, that only those who are handicapped by ill-health or in some other way are likely to adopt the philosophic life, contenting themselves with the less immediately vivid satisfactions of the looker-on. Is it fanciful to find in John Locke an example of the justice of this remark? After being privately tutored, Locke entered Westminster School at the age of fourteen; and taking one year longer than the usual curriculum of five years, did not proceed to Oxford until he was in his twenty-first year. There he continued his linguistic and other studies, following out what seems to have been his first intention, or at least his father's intention, of preparing himself for the Church. He early came to have doubts as to whether this was his proper calling, but it was not until 1666, when he was thirty-four years of age, that he finally abandoned all thoughts of it. Meantime, thanks to his intimacy with Boyle and his scientific circle, he had become interested in the physical sciences, and especially in their practical application in medicine; and as these new interests gained upon him, he resolved to become a physician.

Whereas up to this point we have no information as to Locke's general health, we may reasonably suppose that it had been somewhat delicate, handicapping him in many ways, accounting for his late entry to the University, and so abating his energies as to prevent his earlier adoption of a permanent profession. We hear nothing of any sudden failure of health, but from 1666 onwards there are constant references in his correspondence to his ailments; and notwithstanding the anxious care of devoted friends, these infirmities were his constant companions through all his later years. They constrained him again to change his programme of life. As Lady Masham—the source of our most intimate knowledge of Locke—tells us: "Some time after that Mr. Locke had begun to study in earnest, he applied himself principally to physic—a science which he yet never afterwards made use of to his profit, as not being well able to bear the fatigue those must undergo who would bring themselves into any considerable practice."

Happily, at this juncture, a new way of life, highly congenial to him, and consistent with his poor health, was suddenly opened out by a chance meeting with Lord Ashley, afterwards the first Earl of Shaftesbury. The meeting resulted in their becoming life-long friends. Lord Ashley installed Locke in his London house, in the Strand, as his private physician and as tutor to his son; and later when he became President of the Board of Trade and Lord Chancellor, from 1672 onwards, as a trusted secretary and adviser in his political concerns. Locke also received a Government appointment as Secretary of Presentations (to benefices), and later as Secretary to the Council of Trade and Foreign Plantations. Thus far, Locke's health, though troublesome, had sufficed for these varied calls upon his energies. It gradually worsened, however; and in 1675 he went into retirement in France, where he spent three years, partly in Paris, chiefly in Montpellier. Writing to a friend from Paris in 1677 he says: "My health is the only mistress I have a long time courted, and is so coy a one that I think it will take up the remainder of my days to obtain her good graces and keep her in good humour." [1]

On his return to England Locke was again engaged with Shaftesbury in political activities of various kinds; but sharing in the consequences of his fall from power, he followed him into exile in Holland. And so at last, in the enforced inactivities of a life at once of ill-health and of exile, he became, what otherwise the preoccupations of active life would probably never have permitted, a professional thinker and writer on philosophical subjects, his first work appearing some seven years later, when he was fifty-eight years of age.

[1] Fox Bourne, *Life of John Locke*, I, p. 370.

There was one later occasion on which the enticements of practical life again presented themselves. In returning to England in February 1689 in the train of King William, he was offered the Ambassadorship to the Court of Frederick the First, Elector of Brandenburg, one of the most important positions in the diplomatic service, Frederick being the ally on whom William had mainly to rely in his opposition to Louis XIV. But Locke's good genius, in the guise of ill-health, again, happily for Philosophy, entered an interdict. His letter of refusal, addressed to Lord Mordaunt, has survived, and contains these passages: "I cannot but in the highest degree be sensible of the great honour his Majesty has done me in those gracious intentions towards me which I have understood from your Lordship; and it is the most touching displeasure I have ever received from that weak and broken constitution of my health which has so long threatened my life, that it now affords me not a body suitable to my mind in so desirable an occasion of serving his Majesty . . . My Lord, the post that is mentioned to me is at this time, if I mistake not, one of the busiest and most important in all Europe. . . . But what shall a man do in the necessity of application and variety of attendance on business to be followed there, who sometimes after a little motion has not breath to speak, and cannot borrow an hour or two of watching from the night without repaying it with a great waste of time the next day?" [1]

Locke did, indeed, accept the modest office of Commissioner of Appeals, and later very reluctantly agreed to act for a time as one of the Commissioners of the Board of Trade. But save for his occasional visits to London, in discharge of the duties of these offices, the remaining fourteen years of his life were spent in the country, in almost complete retirement, under the devoted care of Lady Masham and her family. And there we can picture him, as he describes himself in a letter to his Quaker friend, Benjamin Furley, resident in Rotterdam: "Do not think now I am grown either a stoic or a mystic. I can laugh as heartily as ever, and be in pain for the public as much

[1] Lord King, *Life of John Locke* (1830 ed.), I, pp. 319-20.

as you. . . . You may easily conclude this written in a chimney corner, in some obscure hole out of the way of the lazy men of this world and I think not the worse for being so, and I pray heartily it may continue as long as I live. I live in fear of the bustlers, and would not have them come near me. Such quiet fellows as you are, that come without drum and trumpet, with whom we can talk upon equal terms and receive some benefit by their company, I should be glad to have in my neighbourhood, or to see sometimes though they come from the other side of the water." [1]

In reviewing Locke's life, there are two points to which I may direct attention: first, the fact that he published nothing under his own name until he published his main work, the *Essay Concerning Human Understanding*, in his fifty-eighth year; and secondly, that almost immediately upon its appearance Locke became the dominant philosophical influence throughout Europe, displacing Descartes —most notably so in France. Why, having delayed so long, did Locke publish at all? And why was his message so immediately influential, once it had been delivered? The answer which we have to give to the first of these questions also affords in part the answer to the second.

Why was Locke so late in finding his vocation? It does not suffice to say that Locke was one of those whose powers mature slowly and late. The main reason seems to have been that, in the very modest estimate which he had formed of his abilities, he had never been tempted to picture himself as destined to be a leader in the world of thought. Time and again, in his correspondence and writings, we find him protesting with obvious sincerity, that any merit his writings might have was not due to unusual abilities. This unawareness of his powers may, in part, have been caused by the uncongeniality of the linguistic studies to which he had to devote so large a proportion of his time at school and in Oxford, and to the bewilderment of mind occasioned by the scholastic philosophy into which his not very competent teachers sought to initiate him. One of the consolations which he drew from his first eager reading

[1] Fox Bourne, *op. cit.*, II, p. 506.

of Descartes was that perhaps, after all, this had not proceeded from any defect in his understanding, since however often he might differ in opinion from Descartes, he never failed to find him intelligible.

Fortunately Locke early acquired the habit—so much more usual than in these modern days—of writing out his views on any topic that might interest him, and of communicating them in epistolary form to his friends. While at Oxford, he was not, Lady Masham tells us, "any very hard student," but "sought the company of pleasant and witty men, with whom he likewise took great delight in corresponding by letters, and in conversation and these correspondences he spent for some years much of his time." Practically all his writings originated in this way. It was the appreciative response of his friends, and their urgent petitions that these papers be used for the instruction of the world at large, that alone ultimately induced Locke to venture upon publication. In this regard the origins of his *Essay Concerning Human Understanding* are typical. Five or six of his friends, he tells us, meeting at his chamber, and discoursing on a subject very remote from that of the *Essay*—as we know from one of these friends they were discussing the "principles of morality and revealed religion"—found themselves quickly at a stand by the difficulties that rose on every side. "After we had a while puzzled ourselves . . . it came into my thoughts, that we took a wrong course; and that before we set ourselves upon enquiries of that nature, it was necessary to examine our own abilities, and see what objects our understandings were or were not fitted to deal with. . . . Some hasty and undigested thoughts . . . which I set down against our next meeting, gave the first entrance into this discourse, which being thus begun by chance, *was continued by entreaty*; written by incoherent parcels; and after long intervals of neglect, resumed again, as my humour or occasions permitted; and at last, in a retirement, where an attendance upon my health gave me leisure, was brought into that order thou now seest it." [1] And Locke, addressing his Reader, proceeds: "It will possibly be censured as a great

[1] *Essay: Epistle to the Reader.*

piece of vanity or insolence in me to pretend to instruct this our knowing age, it amounting to little less when I own that I publish this *Essay* with hopes it may be useful to others.   If I have not the luck to please, yet nobody ought to be offended with me.   I plainly tell all my readers, except half a dozen, this treatise was not at first intended for them; and therefore they need not be at the trouble to be of that number . . . I shall always have the satisfaction to have aimed sincerely at truth and usefulness, though in one of the meanest ways. . . .   Everyone must not hope to be a Boyle or a Sydenham; . . . it is ambition enough to be employed as an under-labourer in clearing the ground a little, and removing some of the rubbish that lies in the way to knowledge."

Locke's own account of the origins of the *Essay* is, however, incomplete, and can now be supplemented.   An early draft of the *Essay* was discovered a few years ago by Dr. Benjamin Rand in the Lovelace collection of the Locke manuscripts, and is now accessible in the edition which he published last year.   The meeting of friends, as we previously knew, was in and about the year 1670.   What is a matter of considerable interest, and in view of Locke's own utterances, very unexpected, is that this early draft, which is in Locke's own handwriting and dated by him 1671, and which is about one-tenth the length of the *Essay*, treats in consecutive form, though in a somewhat different order, nearly all the problems later dealt with in the four books into which he divided the *Essay*, and that all his main doctrines are already at this early date more or less definitely formulated.   It is therefore the more surprising that Locke should not have thought of publication until some nineteen years later.   We hear of him rewriting and extending this material during his stay at Montpellier. He showed his manuscript to friends; and Lord Shaftesbury had read it prior to his death, which took place in 1683. But it was subsequently to that date, during his exile in Holland, that Locke made his final revisions and additions. In all probability, Lady Masham declares, the work never would have been finished had he continued in England.[1]

[1] Fox Bourne, *op. cit.*, II, p. 16.

It was, not unlikely, the importunity of his friend Leclerc, whom he first met during his exile in Holland, that finally overcame his disinclination to publish. Leclerc was the editor of a literary and scientific review, entitled the *Bibliotheque Universelle*. For this journal he succeeded in obtaining from Locke a few minor contributions,[1] and finally an outline of the *Essay*. This outline, in the French translation made by Leclerc himself, appeared in January 1687–8; and its reception so encouraged Locke that two years later, in 1690, he published the *Essay* in its complete form. As I have said, it was an immediate success, new editions being called for in rapid succession. It was at once adopted as a text-book at Trinity College, Dublin, where some years later it was studied by Berkeley. With Locke's approval an abridgement of it was prepared by John Wynne, afterwards Bishop of St. Asaph. The decision of the Heads of Colleges in Oxford in 1703 that tutors must not read it with their pupils is even better evidence of the interest which it had aroused. On hearing of the interdict, Locke wrote to his young friend, Anthony Collins: "I take what has been done as a recommendation of that book to the world, as you do, and I conclude, when you and I next meet, we shall be merry upon the subject. For this is certain that, because some wink or turn their heads away, and will not see, others will not consent to have their eyes put out."[2] The French translation of the *Essay*, by Pierre Coste, appeared in 1700; and the Latin translation——Latin we have to bear in mind was then still the language of the learned world——begun in 1696, appeared in 1701. Meantime Locke had been publishing his other writings: his *Letters on Toleration*, his works on Government, on Education, and on Religion.

But while the welcome accorded to the *Essay* was sufficiently encouraging to dispel any doubts that Locke may still have entertained as to his vocation, he would have been amazed, and probably more dismayed than gratified, had he lived to read the eulogies which were passed upon his writings on the Continent, and especially in France, in

[1] cf. Fox Bourne, *op. cit.*, II, pp. 44–5.
[2] Fox Bourne, *op cit.*, II, p. 523.

those formative decades in which Voltaire, Montesquieu, D'Alembert, Diderot, Condillac, and Rousseau were the outstanding figures. They one and all looked up to Locke as the philosopher in whose steps they were proud to follow. He is hailed as "the wise Locke," the "greatest of all philosophers since Plato." Voltaire, in popularizing Newton's discoveries in optics and in astronomy, sought also to popularize the teaching of the *Essay*. "Many," he says, and among them he included Descartes, "have written the romance of the mind; a sage has come who has modestly written its history." The Abbé de Condillac wrote his *Essay on the Origin of Human Knowledge* as a supplement to Locke's *Essay*. D'Alembert, in the *Discourse* with which he prefaces the first volume of the great *Encyclopædie*, claims for Locke that he had created metaphysics very much as Newton had created physics. In paying this tribute to Locke, D'Alembert is not, in any unpatriotic spirit, forgetting Descartes. Descartes he depicts as the great geometer, and as the protagonist of reason, liberating the European mind, as no other had done, from the yoke of tradition and authority, and yet all the while forging weapons that in the end had to be turned against himself—his positive teaching with its many reactionary doctrines having to yield place to the counter-teaching of Locke.

This strain of eulogy continued unabated, in France at least, throughout the century. As late as 1794, in Condorcet's posthumously published work, *An Historical View of the Progress of the Human Mind*, a work of which the National Assembly ordered three thousand copies to be printed at the public expense, we find Condorcet describing what he takes to be the new method first formulated by Locke, and which he roundly declares to have been the method to which all genuine philosophical thinking, alike in the physical and in the moral sciences, has since conformed. While it was mainly Locke's *Essay*, it was not solely the *Essay* that earned for him this position of preeminence; his writings on toleration and government, on education, and on religion also played their part. Montesquieu in questions of government, and Rousseau in treating of education, bear witness to their indebtedness to him. Those who set themselves in opposition to the prevailing spirit of the times entertained of course no such reverence for Locke; but even they paid indirect homage to his influence by the violence of their denunciations. This is especially true of De Maistre; he depicts Locke as "the evil genius" of the eighteenth century.

To proceed therefore to our second question: How came Locke—in such complete contrast to the neglect, and even obloquy, that awaited his predecessor Hobbes and his con temporary Spinoza—how came he to exert, in so short a space of time after the appearance of the *Essay*, a European influence of the first magnitude, and also to retain it over so long a period? Was this not a strange fate to befall so modest and so moderate a writer? Certainly it calls for explanation; and the explanation, which is not far to seek, would seem to be mainly twofold: on the one hand the *representative* character of Locke's teaching, and on the other hand, the relations in which he stood to Descartes and to Newton.

Let us consider each of these two points in turn. In the course of his life Locke enjoyed an extraordinary range of varied experiences. "I no sooner perceived myself in the world," he wrote in 1660, "but I found myself in a storm which has lasted hitherto." When he was a boy of ten, the Civil War was raging around his home in Bristol; and political troubles again came very near him when King Charles was beheaded within a few hundred yards of the school in which he was a pupil. Prayers were said that morning in the school for the preservation of the life of the King. While at first Locke, like his Father, had Puritan sympathies, many of his friends were Royalists; and he was caught up into the vortex of their competing interests, learning by bitter experience that the Presbyterians and the Independents, in coming to power, could be just as intolerant as the most extreme of their opponents. Welcoming the Restoration, he found opportunity, in the service of the Earl of Shaftesbury, to acquire first-hand experience in the management of public affairs, and this from a point of vantage which enabled him to follow their course, with first-hand knowledge of the issues and personalities involved. Partly in the service of the State and partly, as we have seen, for reasons of health, he travelled and resided in France, in Germany, and as an exile in Holland, his keen mind eager and open to almost every human interest. Even when politically engaged, he maintained the scientific and other contacts which had been formed in Oxford and elsewhere, corresponding on all kinds of topics with a large circle of friends. In particular he very early came to stand in intimate personal relations with the chief scientific workers of his time. The scientific group which was concerned in the Founding of the Royal Society, the group of which Boyle was the centre, occasionally met in Locke's rooms in Oxford. Locke was himself elected a Fellow of the Society in 1668; and presumably it was at its meetings that he first became acquainted with Newton. After Boyle's death Locke edited Boyle's *General History of the Air*, a work which Boyle had started at Locke's instigation, and for which Locke had himself made observations.

But, of course, it was not only Locke's general interest, however intelligent, in all these matters, that gave its characteristic cast to his thinking. We must never forget that to his friends and acquaintances he was Dr. Locke, that he had very thoroughly equipped himself to be a practising physician, and that throughout his life he practised the art from time to time, placing his knowledge and skill freely at the disposal of his friends. When Shaftesbury had to undergo a delicate and difficult operation, it was upon Locke's judgment and practical skill that he chose to rely. Was some acquaintance in despair over persistent ill-health, or did he have a child that was sickly, it was to Locke, sooner or later, that appeal for aid and advice came to be made. His knowledge of methods of treatment and of the effects of drugs, and still more of diet, he was constantly adding to, with the consequence that the bodily conditions of our human existence were never in danger of being lost sight of when as a philosopher he came to speculate on the nature and limits of the human understanding or to formulate views on education and on government.

Thus we are, I think, justified in maintaining that Locke

was quite peculiarly equipped to appreciate the specific needs and the major tendencies of his age, equipped as no other contemporary thinker could claim to be; and that this is, therefore, one very obvious explanation of the welcome accorded to his writings. But these considerations, relevant and important as they are, by no means suffice to answer our question. Locke could never have gained so immediate and so universal a welcome in England and throughout Europe had it not been for the favouring relations in which, thanks to historical contingencies, he happened to stand to the two great figures of the philosophy and science of his time, namely to Descartes and to Newton. Like two great planets in conjunction, they created the tide that swept Locke's venturing argosies into so many foreign ports.

Though Locke gained his first relish for philosophical enquiry from Descartes, his interest in the empirical sciences, and especially his medical studies, enabled him to adopt, from the very start, a critical and detached attitude towards Descartes' teaching. In particular, they acted as a prophylactic, guarding Locke against any temptation to regard as satisfactory its dualistic foundations. He insisted that man is not to be understood apart from the body, that the problem of the interrelation of mind and body, in its metaphysical aspects, has for us no very special urgency; and in consequence he set aside, as of little value, almost the whole of Descartes' metaphysics. What, on the other hand, he gratefully adopted from Descartes, his doctrine of clear and distinct ideas, and his rationalist method of approach to all problems, are precisely those features in Descartes' philosophy that allowed of a general welcome, especially when, as in Locke, they were supplemented by due recognition, so completely absent in Descartes, of the part which experience must play in providing the materials with which reason has to cope. Since Locke could thus take over all those elements in Descartes' philosophy which were suited to the needs of his contemporaries, and also was able, in place of much that Descartes had retained from the older ways of thinking, to substitute doctrines more in keeping with the scientific and other tendencies of the times, it is not surprising that the Cartesian philosophy put up so poor a fight, and everywhere yielded place, not least quickly and completely in France itself, to Locke's type of teaching.

In yet another regard Locke is a carrier of Cartesian doctrine, namely, in his insistence upon the necessity of new beginnings, through an abrupt break with the past. Alike in Descartes and in Locke, this takes the form of a depreciatory estimate of the value both of history and of learning. Truth, they argue, is independent of time. To engage our energies in study of the ever-changing opinions and beliefs of men is therefore worse than useless; when truth is our goal, to carry a weight of learning is to be handicapped in the race with the simple and the merely ignorant. Fired by this conviction, Descartes and Locke lived provincially in the age to which they belonged; and in respect of the many prejudices and limitations to which their teaching became thereby subject, neither had the advantage over the other. In the century that followed—a century even less historically minded than the seventeenth—no small part of Locke's influence was due to his unquestioning adherence to this way of thinking.

The history of seventeenth-century science reads, as Whitehead has said, "as though it were some vivid dream of Plato or Pythagoras." [1] Starting with Descartes' creation of analytic geometry, the mathematical sciences, entering upon a period of extraordinarily fruitful development, had given rise to the most extravagant hopes that by analogous methods metaphysics might be enabled to make corresponding advances. Such, indeed, is the philosophical ideal for which Descartes stood, or rather, since this statement is not wholly just, it is the ideal to which Descartes' successors believed him to be committed. Descartes was conceived as the great geometer, and as teaching that philosophy must itself be geometrical in method, that it is in a position to start from principles which are guaranteed by reason, and which, when followed by reason into their necessary consequences, place in our hands the keys adequate to the solution of all the problems of

[1] *Science and the Modern World*, p. 46.

science and philosophy. This interpretation of Descartes' purposes is, as I have just suggested, unfair to him; but it is by no means so unfair, if the spirit of his teaching be gathered from the programme which he set himself in physics and astronomy. And, as it happened, it was almost exclusively by his teaching in these fields that his philosophy as a whole came to be judged.

The subsequent course of events, which was highly dramatic, is quite unintelligible save in the light of the dominant influence exercised by Newton, an influence which in philosophy no less than in science has all the importance of a watershed dividing two epochs from one another. Notwithstanding the character of the work done by Kepler, Galileo and Huyghens—all of whom were concerned with the problems of applied mathematics—prior to Newton it was still possible to argue, in the Cartesian manner, that the mathematical ideal of a purely deductive science is the ideal also for physical science, and that it is possible of early achievement. To this somewhat superficial type of rationalism Newton, through his discoveries in optics and in astronomy, gave—at least so far as the next two centuries were concerned—what was virtually the death-blow, the issue being decided in the great controversy between the Newtonian and the Cartesian types of cosmology. Thanks to Voltaire, it became a hotly debated subject among the intelligent public. Descartes professed to have demonstrated *"by means of reason"* [1] that light must be so and so constituted and is instantaneous in its action; Newton *"by means of a prism"* proved that in actual fact it is quite otherwise constituted and takes (on his estimate) six and a half minutes in travelling to us from the sun. Descartes professed to show *"by the natural light of reason"* that there must be vortices of subtle matter, and that in these vortices is to be found the explanation of the movements of the planets; Newton *"by observations upon comets"* proved that there are in actual fact no such vortices. Newton thus made clear beyond all questioning, that however important be the part played by mathematics in physical enquiry, observation and experiment are no less

[1] Voltaire's *Lettres Philosophiques*, Letters XIV, XV and XVI.

indispensable as supplying the brute data, the "irreducible and stubborn facts," which reason may not ignore and is required to interpret.

Whitehead has asserted [1] that in consequence of this revolution the men of science became anti-rationalist, being content with a simple faith in the order of nature, and that it was the clergy alone who continued to uphold the rights of reason. But this, surely, is a perverse reading of what actually happened. The typical thinkers of the eighteenth century are, indeed, in striking contrast to those of the seventeenth century, *anti-metaphysical*; but this did not in the least weaken their conviction that in all matters of controversy reason is the sole ultimate court of appeal. What they had come to recognize—and it is here that Locke, following Newton, seemed to them to have shown the way —was that while reason is the instrument, it is never in and by itself a source of insight; and that speculation is therefore idle save when we are constrained to it in our efforts to define what it is that is being vouched for by experience.

Newton's *Principia*, it is important to remember, appeared just four years prior to Locke's *Essay*. Being at one in the empirical character of their teaching as in the time of their publication, they came to be associated in men's minds, each work assisting in the spread of the other. And in this partnership it was, of course, Locke who stood to be the main beneficiary. The battle-cry which Voltaire adopted in his great crusade was: "the Newtonian Philosophy and Locke as its Prophet."

To return for a moment to the subject of my original question—Locke's vogue in France throughout the eighteenth century. When we bear in mind what Descartes has meant, and still means, to the French people, as giving classical expression to so much that is native to their genius, it seems strangely paradoxical that an Englishman, and so very English an Englishman as John Locke, should have been allowed, for the space of a century, to eclipse in their esteem their own native teacher—a teacher who, as we must admit, is the greater figure of the two. But the

[1] *Science and the Modern World*, p. 73.

paradox is more seeming than real. As I have already said, Locke took over from Descartes precisely those elements in his teaching which were suited to the needs of the times, his insistence on clear and distinct ideas, and his trust in reason as exercising supreme sovereignty in all matters of controversy. Locke re-stated these doctrines in the manner demanded by the results of the empirical sciences, and especially of Newton's great discoveries. Thereby Locke became the chief channel through which all that could be immediately fruitful in Descartes' teaching came to its own; and it was these parts of Locke's Philosophy that alone gained general currency in France. The Locke they adopted was not the complete Locke, but Locke cut to a French pattern, as befitted the rôle assigned to him. It is accordingly no exaggeration to say that what France, in the eighteenth century, received from England at the hands of Locke is in large part what France, in the seventeenth century, had herself given to England, in the person of Descartes. In substituting Locke the philosopher for Descartes the metaphysician, the French were not therefore proving false to their own traditions; they were conserving them, and this in a manner which allowed their realist aptitudes—surely no less typical of the French genius —to gain more adequate expression than was possible within the limits of the Cartesian system.

In the comedy of human life time plays strange tricks with men and affairs. Here we have Locke, the most modest of men, being set on a pedestal as a rival to Plato, or when attacked by his enemies treated as an influence so powerful as to have poisoned the mind of a whole century. That Locke should have lent himself to such apotheosis and attack, is easily understandable as regards his controversial writings—Locke the protagonist of toleration, Locke as standing for constitutional rights and for individual liberty, and for a simplified theology, Locke the educationalist, Locke the opponent of innate ideas in the first book of the *Essay*. It was natural that the importance of these writings should be overestimated. Just because of their immediate serviceableness, being written to meet contemporary needs, nothing in them was likely to fail of effect.

But as regards the *Essay*, outside the first book, only a few of its main doctrines, not always those that we should now regard as the most important, received attention; and as a rule these were formulated in some doctrinaire manner, quite contrary to the temperate, tentative, qualified spirit in which they were put forward by Locke himself. Accordingly the passing away of the eighteenth-century overestimate of Locke has not, so far as the *Essay* is concerned, brought any excessive reaction in its train. On the contrary, when the clouds of incense ceased to rise, in place of the cosmopolitan figure, there emerged the plain honest features of the genuine Locke, less imposing but more individual, distinctively English, and with a great deal more in his teaching than the eighteenth century, notwithstanding its exaggerated worship of him, had ever been sufficiently interested to study and appreciate.

Let us then, in the time that remains, turn to the complete Locke, the English Locke, as he reveals himself to us in his writings, and especially in the *Essay*. No one can read these writings without being struck by the predominance of the moral note. Sober and discriminating in all his judgments, he tested everything by a twofold criterion, truth and usefulness, neither, as he seems to have believed, being possible in the absence of the other. On first hearing, this may seem to be a somewhat commonplace and prosaic creed; it is redeemed by the freshness and liberality, no less than by the religious intensity, with which Locke held it. "It is a duty we owe to God, as the fountain and author of all truth, who is truth itself; and it is a duty also we owe our own selves, if we will deal candidly and sincerely with our own souls, to have our minds constantly disposed to entertain and receive truth wheresoever we meet with it, and under whatsoever appearance of plain or ordinary, strange, new, or perhaps displeasing, it may come in our way. Truth is the proper object, the proper riches and furniture of the mind, and according as his stock of this is, so is the difference and value of one man above another. . . . Our first and great duty then is, to bring to our studies and to our enquiries after knowledge a mind covetous of truth; that seeks after nothing else, and after that impartially, and embraces it, how poor, how contemptible, how unfashionable soever it may seem."[1]   For Locke truth is no mere abstract term; it came to him weighted with the benefits and powers that, as he believed, may confidently be counted to follow in its train.

No less characteristic of Locke's writings are certain features which I may perhaps not unfairly describe as distinctively English, moderation, preference for qualified over unqualified statement, for adequacy over consistency, distrust of logic so long as contrary facts are in evidence, and consequent comparative lack of interest in the more metaphysical aspects of philosophy.   These characteristics have been very happily summed up by Professor S. Alexander. "[The] general tone [of Locke's writings] is that of equable common-sense, without emphasis, without enthusiasm, restrained in its judgment, careful of measure, never dull but reflecting evenly from a candid surface, modest when it is most original, because concerned with the faithful presentment of things, rather lambent than fiery, an inspired pedestrianism."[2]

Yet another general characteristic of Locke's teaching —I have already referred to it as common to him and to Descartes—is his insistence that in matters of knowledge and belief each man must stand on his own feet.   "He that distrusts his own judgment in everything, and thinks his understanding not to be relied on in the search of truth, cuts off his own legs that he may be carried up and down by others, and makes himself a ridiculous dependent upon the knowledge of others, which can possibly be of no use to him; for I can no more know anything by another man's understanding than I can see by another man's eyes."[3] Why, Locke asks, "make it one's business to study what have been other men's sentiments in things where reason is only to be judge?"[4]   The teaching which Locke thus inculcated he himself practised, and to it his philosophy owes many of its chief merits, and some of its defects.   He lived almost entirely in his time, reading, for the most part,

[1] Lord King, *op. cit.*, I, pp. 187–8.   [2] *Locke* (1908), p. 23.
[3] Lord King, *op. cit.*, I, p. 196.   [4] *Op. cit.*, I, p. 175.

the works only of his contemporaries, and even these but
sparingly. Every field in which he worked he prospected
as if it were virgin country, never before explored. This,
indeed, is the key-note of all Locke's writings, no matter
on what topic he may be writing: not that he himself
made extravagant claims to originality—that he left to his
eighteenth-century eulogists. "He who has raised himself above the alms-basket, and not content to live lazily
on scraps of begged opinions, sets his own thoughts on
work, to find and follow truth, will (whatever he lights on)
not miss the hunter's satisfaction; every moment of his
pursuit will reward his pains with some delight, and he
will have reason to think his time not ill-spent, even when
he cannot much boast of any great acquisition." [1]

Take, for instance, Locke's *Thoughts Concerning Education*.
Here indeed was a virgin territory, for Locke the physician,
for Locke who looked back with such regrets upon the
opportunities that his teachers had failed to open out to
him, for Locke the lover, and himself the especial favourite,
of children. Consider some of the many novel maxims
that he propounds. That children should live much in
the open air, and should go bareheaded; that it is custom
alone that makes children more liable to catch cold through
the feet than through the hands, and that their shoes should
therefore be so constructed that they do *not* keep out the
wet—in a word, the present-day sandals; that the ideal
breakfast for children is plain brown bread, preferably
without butter, and small beer; that children be not too
warmly clad, winter or summer; that their beds be hard and
made in different fashions, the pillow now high and now
low, that they may not in after-life be put out when something is amiss. "The great cordial is sleep. He that
misses that, will suffer by it; and he is very unfortunate
who can take his cordial only in his mother's fine gilt cup,
and not in a wooden dish." Nor is Locke above dwelling
upon the evils of costiveness, and the duty of paying
"court"—as he expresses it—"to Madame Cloacina." "It
being an indisposition I had a particular reason to enquire
into, and not finding the cure of it in books, I set my

[1] *Essay: Epistle to the Reader.*

thoughts on work, believing that greater changes than that might be made in our bodies, if we took the right course, and proceeded by rational steps."

In things of the mind, the formation of character, he holds, takes first place. Next in importance he reckons wisdom in the management of affairs; third he places good-breeding; and only thereafter book-learning. Dancing he regards as a main instrument of education; and would have children disciplined by its means from their earliest years. "For, though this consist only in outward gracefulness of motion, yet, I know not how, it gives children manly thoughts and carriage, more than anything." The ordinary school curriculum, as he had himself known it, he regarded with little favour. "What ado," he says, "is made about a little Latin and Greek, how many years are spent in it, and what a noise and business it makes to no purpose." But the defender of the classics will be apt to think that Locke, in his candour, weakens his case, in disclosing his mind somewhat further. "If [a child] have a poetic vein, it is to me the strangest thing in the world, that the father should desire or suffer it to be cherished or improved. Methinks the parents should labour to have it stifled or suppressed as much as maybe; and I know not what reason a father can have to wish his son a poet, who does not desire to have him bid defiance to all other callings and business . . . for it is very seldom seen that any one discovers mines of gold or silver in Parnassus. It is a pleasant air, but a barren soil; and there are very few instances of those who have added to their patrimony by anything they have reaped from thence." Poetry and the fine arts lay outside the range of Locke's otherwise very catholic interests.

In general, Locke is confident that the road to knowledge can, by new and proper methods, be made short and easy. French and Latin are to be learned by reading and talking. "Latin is no more unknown to a child, when he comes into the world, than English; and yet he learns English without master, rule or grammar; and so might he Latin too as Tully did, if he had somebody always to talk to him in this language." In the curriculum for school and college he would also include the study of the sciences, of law, and of philosophy, but not either rhetoric or logic; and he would give prime importance to the pupils' mother-tongue. Would it, he asks, "be very unreasonable to require a learned schoolmaster (who has all the tropes and figures in Farnaby's rhetoric at his fingers' ends) to teach his scholar to express himself handsomely in English, when it appears to be so little his business or thought, that the boy's mother . . . outdoes him in it?" In addition Locke would have every child learn "a manual trade; if practicable two or three, but one more particularly."

But we should not pass from Locke's work on education without noting what is one of its great qualities, namely his sympathetic understanding of child-life, and his demand that the discipline and training which he recognized to be very necessary be by gentler methods than those which had hitherto prevailed. The article on Locke in Diderot's *Encyclopædie* is unsigned; but internal evidence reveals the author. Who but Rousseau could have written the following passage, which gives a very French version of what is not untrue to the essential spirit of Locke's teaching? "Accustom the mind to the spectacle of nature . . . it is always great and simple. . . . Unhappy the children who have never seen the tears of their parents flow upon the recital of a generous action; unhappy the children who have never seen the tears of their parents flow at the sight of the misfortune of others. Fable relates that Deucalion and Pyrrha repeopled the earth by throwing stones behind them. There remains in the soul of the most sensible something of its stony origins; and we must labour to recognize and to soften it."

Locke's independent approach to every subject that came to occupy his attention can similarly be illustrated in the case of his other writings. These, however, in even greater degree than his *Thoughts Concerning Education*, are now of almost purely historical interest. It is the *Essay Concerning Human Understanding* by which Locke's genius must mainly be judged. It has stood the test of time as no other of his writings has done. His influence throughout the eighteenth century, as I have sought to show, was favoured by circumstances which conferred upon his writings a timeliness and an importance they could not otherwise have had; and there was consequently an element of happy accident in the recognition accorded to Locke. But this cannot be said as regards the present-day reputation of the *Essay*. It has attained the assured rank of a philosophical classic, thanks to the sane, solid, and at the same time original, qualities of Locke's native genius.

The four Books into which the *Essay* is divided are of very unequal value. Books I and III are much shorter than the others, forming between them only one-fourth of the *Essay*. As I have already suggested, Book I is little more than a controversial tract, with almost no present-day relevance. Book III, which treats of language, though expository in character, has also little present value. In it Locke shows no appreciation of the closeness and subtlety of the inter-relations between thought and language. He is merely repeating and applying the kind of views which were then current—that language, while socially indispensable, is from an intellectual point of view a necessary evil, and the prime cause of fallacy—views not unnatural when we bear in mind that the type of philosophy then still dominant in the universities was a weakened form of Scholasticism, which employed an archaic and highly technical phraseology, and which was so out of keeping with the times that even its most reputable teachers had no genuine and living appreciation of the truths for which it stood. The intellectual life, Locke seems to say—as did Berkeley after him—should largely be spent in dodging out of the way of words. I am apt, Locke says, to imagine that when we quit words, and think upon things, we all think the same; whereas when we have some strange, outlandish doctrine to propound, it is upon legions of obscure, doubtful and undefined words that reliance is placed, so that the positions defended are more like the dens of robbers or the holes of foxes than the fortress of truth. This view of language is still occasionally to be met with among workers in the sciences; students of the humanities have, happily, freed themselves from it.

It is, therefore, to the other two Books of the *Essay*, to

Books II and IV, that we have to look for Locke's main contribution to philosophy. What is that contribution? Usually the opening sections of Book II have been given such prominence that Locke's purposes and teaching in the *Essay* have been set in a very misleading light, as if he were mainly intent upon showing that the materials of knowledge are all-important, and are all, without exception, empirically obtained. This is part of the teaching of the *Essay*, but in Locke's own view—and he was entirely justified in so believing—the less important and the less original part. The primary purpose of the *Essay* is to determine the nature, conditions and limits of knowledge, the term "knowledge" being employed in an unusually strict and narrow sense. As Professor Gibson, in his masterly work on *Locke's Theory of Knowledge* has pointed out,[1] for Locke knowledge and certainty are equivalent terms. Knowledge, Locke holds, excludes the possibility not only of doubt but of error. It is a form of absolutely certain cognition; and to possess it is to recognize it as such. "With me," he says, "to know and to be certain is the same thing: what I know, that I am certain of; and what I am certain of, that I know. What reaches to knowledge, I think may be called certainty; and what comes short of certainty, I think cannot be called knowledge." [2]

How, Locke asks, is this knowledge possible; in what fields is it possible; and what are the substitutes for it, where it is not available? Locke believed himself to have quite definite answers to these questions. Knowledge proper, he declares, is scientific; and consists of truths which are abstract and universal. The most *obvious* examples of such knowledge are, he recognizes, to be found in the mathematical sciences. But since "our business here is not to know all things, but those which concern our conduct," it is in "morality" and in "divinity" that we must look for its most *important* instances. Outside these three fields, we have at best only an assurance resting on probabilities—an assurance which for practical purposes may amount to certainty but still never is certainty.

[1] *Op. cit.*, p. 2.
[2] Second Letter to Stillingfleet, *Works*, Vol. IV, p. 145.

Such is the very strange answer that Locke gives to his fundamental question: what is the nature and what are the limits of knowledge? Knowledge, absolutely certain knowledge, is possible in mathematics, in ethics, and in natural theology; it is possible nowhere else. Both physics and metaphysics are excluded from the domain of knowledge; they are concerned with the dark, not with the possibly "enlightened" parts of things; and accordingly they should be pursued no further than practical need compels.

Now had Locke been true to his own programme, had he in the *Essay* consistently held to these positions, and succeeded in formulating a body of teaching in harmony with them, the *Essay* would, by now, have been, like his other writings, of purely historical interest. What he actually achieved, as distinguished from what he believed himself to have achieved, was to show, with admirable force and suggestiveness, that such hard and fast distinctions, such attempts at clear-cut delimitation of the knowable from the unknowable, are far from tenable, and that the metaphysical issues, the discussion of which he has deprecated, are not to be evaded in any such off-hand fashion. This, indeed, is precisely what lends to the *Essay* its permanent value. Locke does more than merely abstain from concealing counter-considerations. He was much too deeply interested in the problems, as problems, to be under any temptation to do other than emphasize them; and for the same reason, the metaphysical issues, though ruled out on principle, receive in the course of the *Essay*, no small share of attention.

All this comes about in the following manner. There is a conflict between the account given in Book II of the origins and nature of our ideas, and the teaching of Book IV, which deals with the validity of the knowledge we have by means of them. In Book II Locke declares sensation and reflection to be the two possible sources of all our ideas, reflection being described as itself a kind of inner sense. To these two sources, he tells us, all our simple ideas are due; we can have no complex ideas that are not reducible, without remainder, to such simple ideas. Yet later in the

Essay, when Locke passes from the consideration of sense-experience to the treatment of knowledge, when, that is to say, he passes from the consideration of how we acquire experience in time to the consideration of truth, which holds independently of time, we find that he traces such knowledge neither to sensation nor to reflection, but to a quite new source of experience, which he entitles "intuition." And patently there is such a third source of experience. The apprehension that two units added to two units make four units is not a set of simple ideas; it is a proposition, the truth of which is learned through direct inspection. In what relation, then, does such direct intuitive inspection stand to sense-experience? Locke's answer is virtually to accentuate the distinction until it becomes an opposition between what is given to the mind and what the mind does for itself, and so paradoxically enough to base truth not on experience but on constructions of which the mind is alleged to be the author. Sense-experience, like the world from which we receive it, is ever-changing and gives, he says, no assurance beyond the moment. Like time it is a perpetual perishing; once past it can never recur. Intuition, on the other hand, yields knowledge that is universal and holds independently of time: a proposition, if true at all, has always been true and must remain true. This difference between our changing sense-experiences and the propositions in which intuition expresses its insights points back, Locke argues, to an equally marked difference in the nature of their objects. Sense-experience is of the real, which as real is always changing and in each of its changing states is inexhaustibly complex. For both reasons, that the real changes and that it is inexhaustibly complex, it is not being known even when it is being experienced. Sense-experience does not carry us beyond the moment of its own occurrence, and even at the moment we apprehend only the simple ideas present to the mind, not the reality to which they are due. Intuitive knowledge, on the other hand, is not of the real but of the abstract, not of the changing but of the immutable, not of terms—that is, not of simple ideas—but of relations which presuppose at least two terms, two ideas.

Indeed it is the relations, and not the terms, the structural features of the compound, and not its separate constituents, of which alone we come to have understanding, when we formulate propositions and recognize them as true.

Thus the objects of intuition are not ideas at all, not at least of any kind allowed for by Locke in his account of the sources of experience. They are immutable essences, each with a complex nature that is no longer itself if any, even the least, alteration be made in it. Locke adds, indeed, that they are essences and not realities, nominal not real, abstract with none of the inexhaustibleness that is proper to the genuinely actual. But while thus seeming to withdraw with one hand what he puts forward with the other, he does not withdraw from either of the two opposed positions, that sense-experience is never knowledge, and that there is a knowledge which is otherwise obtained. The nearest that experience can come to having the certainty proper to knowledge is in experimental sampling and the generalizations based on such sampling; but this, Locke insists, is worlds apart from the certainty attained in mathematical and other intuited propositions.

From logic and the theory of knowledge Locke then leads us on, in his speculations regarding "substance" and what he entitles "*real* essences," to the problems of metaphysics. Is existence, like time, a perpetual perishing; or have we the right to posit what direct experience, in Locke's view, never discloses, a something that survives the passing of time, a something that fulfils itself in and through change? Or to state the problem in a wider form, is the compound resolvable into the simple, is the enduring reducible to the successive; and if so, is the complex and enduring nothing in its own right, is it a mere aggregate or series, without any structure proper and peculiar to itself? To these questions Locke suggests the same antithetic answers as to those we have just been considering. His theory of the sources of experience leads him in one direction, the nature of the knowledge which we actually possess leads him in a quite opposite direction. Thus to read Locke is constantly to be made to question what the

Author is saying in any one passage in the light of what he has said elsewhere, with the result that the *Essay*, when we are studying it, is—is it not?—as often on the knee as in the hand. And is not this the best tribute that a reader can pay to a reflective work of this kind?

To employ a distinction drawn by Whitehead, what we have come to value in Locke's *Essay* is his adequacy, an adequacy constantly obtained in disregard of consistency. He opens out fundamental problems in a manner none the less admirable that quite patently he fails to afford an answer that is final or satisfactory. This, under the circumstances, is a positive merit. For the questions, which he sets us asking are problems which, as we have to recognize, still retain their central position, and to which, after two centuries of philosophical speculation, there is still no agreed solution. In respect of this considered, balanced, weighty character of its teaching, the *Essay* stands apart from Locke's other writings. As we have seen, it was Locke's main interest for a period of thirty years, from the time when he first drafted it in 1671 to the year 1700, when he made his final revisions for its fourth edition. Compared with the *Essay*, his other writings—with the possible exception of his second *Treatise of Government*—might almost be said to be in the nature of *parerga*. They are propagandist in character, and are seldom elaborated beyond what the immediate needs of the contemporary audience for which they were written seemed to him to demand.

The account which I have given of Locke in this lecture is, I need hardly say, very far from complete, even as an outline. I have barely touched on his writings on religion and on government, and have entirely passed over his writings on finance and currency. I have said nothing about his influence on Berkeley, on Hume, on the Mills and Herbert Spencer, or of the manner in which his *Essay* has contributed to the establishment of psychology as a positive science. I have preferred to dwell on those features of his personality and of his time which enable us to understand how so immense a range of influence has fallen to the lot of a writer so moderate, so candid, so unpreten-

JOHN LOCKE

tious; and why, in especial, his *Essay Concerning Human Understanding* has acquired the unquestioned status of a philosophical classic, each succeeding generation of readers, not least so in these present days, finding in its pages something suited to its needs.

Printed in Great Britain by Butler & Tanner Ltd., Frome and London

PREVIOUS ADAMSON LECTURES

Published by the

MANCHESTER UNIVERSITY PRESS

❧

ON THE LIGHT THROWN BY RECENT IN-VESTIGATIONS ON ELECTRICITY ON THE RELATION BETWEEN MATTER AND ETHER

By Sir J. J. Thomson, O.M., D.Sc., F.R.S. Royal 8vo, paper covers, 6*d*. net.

LEIBNIZ AS A POLITICIAN

By Sir A. W. Ward, Litt.D., F.B.A. Royal 8vo, paper covers, 6*d*. net.

THE DISTINCTION BETWEEN MIND AND ITS OBJECTS

By Bernard Bosanquet, M.A., D.C.L., F.B.A. Crown 8vo, paper covers, 2*s*. net.

ART AND THE MATERIAL

By Samuel Alexander, O.M., LL.D., F.B.A. Crown 8vo, paper covers, 1*s*. 6*d*. net; cloth, 3*s*. net.

❧

23 LIME GROVE,

OXFORD ROAD, MANCHESTER

CPSIA information can be obtained
at www.ICGtesting.com
Printed in the USA
BVHW051416150621
609530BV00004B/346